Tourism industry in 22nd century

Forget the bags
Pythagoraclid

Next trends

- Tourism industry is default combo of entertainment and every sector in the interests of living style space for future
- It's not far from trillion-zillion transition to open tremendous scope of technology changes and economic development meeting the smallest and largest needs of our industry.

Hospitality experience

- Renew the experience of reaching home, with the new or old customer entering the room in your service apartment or hotel or vehicle.
- Let the best be done by your customer and be in easy accessibility to respond to questions.

Related sectors

- Tourism and travel
- Food
- Cultural heritage (clothing, accessories, monuments, communication methods, entertainment)
- Health (most crucial and critical because of no option to user/patient, loophole to exploitation)

Fresh thread

- Same language and dialect communication
- Similar food preparation as at customer home
- Room decoration and ambience replication of visitor preference
- Facilitating the customer in different ways feasible and possible

Travel loopholes

- Do away with limited agent and middleman system for ticketing, guided tours and transfers
- Safety and integrity of both service providers and availors (chaffeurs, self-drivers, et al)
- General information and cooperation of locals
- Currencies at the time of departure should balance out the losses of tourists.

Intermediary leaves

- Some tourists leave earlier to be free of any unexpected hassle or cost
- Some plan intermittent short tours to cover multiple places at multiple times
- Design your offer accordingly

Uninspiring passengers

- Provide easy accessibility, reasonable checking, great offers to passengers who complain about things, know their trouble with giving the opportunity to best serve your esteemed customers because they're sure to inspire you later if you do that today.

Tourists are nodes

- NLP says that tourists can be found to emanate the best outside impressions of a nation and they're malleable to be positively repositioned by your hospitality industry attempts to raise the standards as activity with nodes of global relevance.

Tourism is directly marketing

- The best way to treat tourists is a hospitality as customers to your national interest and support their aspirations because this is a direct marketing opportunity with great costfree impact of self-motivated tourists buying into the international industry trends.

Tourism is financing

- Tourists are spontaneous sources of funding for forex market without any risks and conditions

Tourism is supplying chain of Zen

- The best example of transportation, hotel, restaurant, scenic and ancient riches, cultural surprise, currency wonders, privileges and immunities to the complete value chain analysis leading to the rest of the sectors in economy (entertainment, FMCG, metal, auto, communication, beauty, heavy industries)

Tourism and food chemistry

- Means of transportation, accommodation and communication may be globalised
- Food is purely cultural and renders historical influence on the above domestic impression
- Some plan to correlate the above two could brand you as unique country in the eyes of tourists.

Tourism and apparel industry

- Visitors can relate to your favorable national interest by the attires bought into their country once they get back home so put messages and design of significant and highly effective impact rather than junkies boasting of global uniform in known brands, it's great to offer local native dresses in use.

Tourism and cultural distance

- Different opportunities can be customised based on cultural differences by hovering around the best experiences to exceed expectations of the visitors. Hofstede can come to rescue or cross national experts can guide to get the best tourism innovation.

Tourism and economic plan

- The best way to develop economy is to send welcoming signals to investors, regulators and other participants in the other countries via the tourists landing in the focal country. Ofcourse the actual policy has to be friendly and approachable for the foreigners.

Tourism and globalisation

- Play on the rules of globalisation to get the best of direct linkage between the two, benefits of global tourists can be found to emanate efforts and effects to the rest of the sectors in economy and society of engineering the social mechanisms of globalisation tactics to achieve the best way to get a new product development idea each time you are having great tourism innovation and experience.

Tourism and self

- The industry itself is a great choice for other sub-sectors which are influenced by the single individual to unit firm to sectors complementing and supplementing with products like memento, regional customised clothing, packed food, etc.

Tourism and book industry

- Books and other literature about the new regional specialties can help with unbiased info for tourists
- Even tourists share experiences by writing book
- Books are best friends forever to anyone.
- Book is basic outline opening knittygritties for the visitors.

Tourism and publishing

- Books, websites, blogs, and other digital information and photos are having great demand for tourists
- Redundant data and statistics are also circulating all over the web

Tourism and technology

- The hi tech tourism saves time.
- Make it more traveller-friendly and safe
- Bring tourism spot to home with innovation
- Save travel and accommodation costs by mobile tents and rental space within or near the transportation vehicles.

Tourism helps

- Overcome fear of saturation that comes to benefit of the happy travelers, competing facilities, globalising economy and pacing opportunities
- Improve the national esteem and boost the investment flows through transition to employment and fund ecosystem for host, guest and interactive nations

Employment and tourism

- Guides and other positions are open to the cross-border global citizen in the sectors of hospitality, linguistics, national specialities, fashion, social networking and other to include the every other industry in the journey of your interaction with the new guests.

Investment and tourism

- Tourists are the first impression holders of your national culture and society moulding according to the convenience of your tourists can send signals to economic agents in the continued success of our trade and investment development partnership.

Tourism and trade

- Both promote each other
- Tourism promises and opens contours to trade and exchange the best produces
- Trade allows visitors to gratify the curiosity in knowing more about the trader nation-state.

Tourism and government

- Public access to transport, WiFi, libraries, guest houses, canteens and other facilities or entertainment modes should be provided to tourists for safety reasons to get the trust of both sides working with further national cooperation for welfare of the global tourists.

Tourism and partnerships

- Enter into trade agreements
- Expand the scope of foreign policy
- Allow the visitors to leave the feedback and act upon it
- Reward and facilitate the participation of cross sector dependence and innovation.

Resources for tourism

- Vehicles, technology, books, guides, kiosks, antiques, museums, films, roadshows, exhibition, seminar, works, currencies, research, lodging, food, cultural beauty, cross sector industry, cosmetics, yesterday's experience, tomorrow's expectations, today's strategy

Drivers to tourism industry

- Visitors security
- Home abroad home environment
- New cultural adaptation
- Supply chain management
- Forex market movements

Transportation and logistics

- Tourists need safe means of transportation and accommodation, uninterrupted methods of communication and interpersonal interactive logistics for facilitating the visitor from each possible perspective and service in use.

Colour the best experience

- The ease of establishing and maintaining interaction with getting desired task completion can be found to shape the tourism experience.
- Provide easy option to rent and return the items required for the stay without conditions.

Tourism strategy

- Reward tourists for teaching you about their country and culture instead of nagging them with your offering or saleables to get deliverables for the national competitiveness and international development that takes care of everything else in this sector.

Creativity and tourism

- Animation and games to entertain the visitors
- Mobile hygiene kiosks
- Instant reward for tourists feedback and articles
- Common permit and long validity across multiple places
- Health care without conditions

Occasions to tourism transformation

- Separate options for pooling with locals and visitors to personal satisfaction
- Combine technology and human services tailored to suit visitors' preference
- Tourism spots should have the same national Heritage represented by every means possible for mutual gain.

Tourism industry is agility natural

- Tours and travels are planned for facilitating the broad and overall logistics but not how we could interact and enjoy, it's a new experience for spontaneous and responsive strategy to grow both visitors and hosts by the relevant sub-sectors to organise the best way for global tourists in managing the needs that you should facilitate much before the consumer comes across.

Competitive tourism

- Multilevel competition in local and national initiatives among other countries to manage but with the new influence of information, technology and facilities for the foreigners for the delight or the best way forward to your favorable impact of self-motivated government support and tourism sector stakeholders.

Technologies to preserve tourism

- Digital audio and visual information to facilitate multilingual interaction with automation and robotics to the extent of overcoming cultural and behavioral drawbacks
- Well maintained government website to every nation's benefit of using blockchain technology for multidimensional information and data communication in assuring tourists of maximum true exhaustive info possible.

Tourism and growth

- Skills and experience can be learnt, moved and grown with the help of tourists in providing the difference between the national ways to improve and develop the best of future dreams
- Join collaborative dealings to advance the ambition of visiting and hosting national citizens of adding to the existing resources.

Give tourists

- Don't expect tourists can do wonders to be donors, and experience the best of your national culture without you offering a new great time and consideration in return for the money and time of visiting guys.

Tourism is not a business

- It's a new friendship and support opportunity for both the visitors and hosts
- The best way forward is to be national champions in furtherance of economic interests and skills of the different countries to manage the intertourism promotion.

Tourism cycle

- Ancient riches develop into cultural heritage
- The inherent invitation and facilities for living with such marvels get the visitors in a specific time or any
- More references and business development
- Unlike other industries there's no direct product and service but natural involvement in ready processed heritage.

Tourism learning curve

- The best of tourism industry is fragmented and unorganised with the street and stall sellers mostly competing with medium sized businesses and few large companies in travel and hospitality that together deal with seasonal business cycle to get growing but low risk of decline and stagnation.

Tourism is more than dynamic

- Different types of people who have a good time, great expectations and new experiences involved in the different parts of value chain manage the intertourism conditions on more dynamic opportunities.

Mobile rooming

- The room is in your bag, to be opened and erected in the allocated space within easy assembly and de-installation, or opting for mobile dens that are provided by company at the short notice but common course is to fix the mobile tents that are immovable and like our standard room.

Don't attach formulae

- Tourists are spontaneous and adventurous
- What is needed is a good understanding of the tourist to give her the best conditions of direct rapport building with the new national culture in every aspect to get a chance to get refined re-evaluation to national championship in cooperation rather than competition.

Possible refinements

- Simplify the process of inspection and movement of tourists in providing specific consideration and consent to the extent of overcoming cultural differences or inhibition of hosts and guests to get a new rapport and trust of getting through accommodation and food adjustments or customisation.

Tourists are not students

- Don't teach tourists in the pretext of providing them with fun and easy enjoyment of earning the tag of the most successful and welcoming host nation but clarify what is allowed and not in your country.

Tourists want home

- Structure of your tourism model must have the same opportunity for local and international participants in the next few growth ventures and the best way forward to providing the home to tourists

Tourism is friendship uninvited

- Tourists are the right back friends that you want but can't obtain as replacement for lost friends and friendship is never forced but natural moreover it is supposed to enrich your good self to mend the poor ways as a total unbiased unrelated foreigner.

Tourism sentiment

- Tourists and visitors have a sentimental value of old or short time to get the satisfaction of learning say from the first presidential antiques, paying tribute to the patriot spot, enjoying the best view of nursery and such things. The hosts and sellers should have the same pride in their products.

Product includes

- Tourism promises, guides, transportation, accommodation, language translation, customised food, international benchmark, news and information technology

Tourism innovation

- Complete guided customised package from the doorstep of visitor's home to the tourism country through each spot on easy terms and totally safe till reaching back home so that you are responsible for the risks and provide delight to the customer.

Promotion

- Tourism and hotel promotion can be customised to your visitors using the best way forward to your package deals and offers to the benefits of global trade in the future

USP

- User should be able to get the best native warmth and comfort in the other countries
- Strategy to grow tourism promises and thanks the best of given heritage and culture of past
- Product includes the best experiences and welcoming tourists in managing the delight.

Health care provider

- The insurance terms should be easier for tourists in managing the multinational travel
- The treatment and health care options should be compatible with tourists
- The best way forward is to encourage the foreign service providers to get the tourists feel like home.

Bring tourism to everyone

- Promote local and international tourism together without discrimination and preferences for local or remote visitors because they're sure to value the efforts on the right development of new product categories to the sector.

Tour your customer

- Traveling with visitors can grow spontaneous feedback to get new ideas for adoption of digital technologies and intelligence software in making interpretation of market transitions early of giving the industry participants chance to repair mistakes.

Man on technology

- Manning on your business technology convincing the visitors of same values in a complete technology implementation can get you restarted for free interaction with customers to switch on the flow of ideas and outputs both sides.

Multiple rivals

- Are there to generate higher visitor quality services that provide simple products or experiments for new business opportunity for important visitor needs of global solutions in Customised service.

Travel

- Should not be sold at Customer getting delight for money Or fun for sale but honest value should be added to get new impact transferred for Customer entertainment or learning with tourism development through coexistence of visitors, service provider and Heritage building agent community.

Delving into future tourism

- Total quality experience and Innovation in accepting the Technology as your culture with value balancing the user attributes in future tourism industry growth of modern relevance by advanced transport mechanisms and flexible accommodation options.

Trend of future

- Tourism and travel industry growth depends upon Customer centric implementation without stopping by goals and Strategies because this sector is faster than imagination with continuous exchanges of service or product range expectations and competitive response.

Futuristic tourist

- Tourist of futuristic modern living is a good user of gadgets and Technological capabilities in furthering the tourism experience to successful balance of providers and consumers at different levels of culture representation in artefact or national assets or Heritage.

Gearing of Customer

- User comes in business picture with needs, stories, observation and perceptions of personal interpretation from the beginning of interaction based project or product management efforts as competing with options for working on new challenges thrown by your customers.

Stages

- Tourist evaluates to select places against the personal needs, fulfills the requirement for travel and daily activities, forms changes in culture during the trip, relives delight that comes out in one form or other feedback.

Foreign exchange

- Not money alone but culture based adaptation of commuters attaining unambiguous innovation in their way of making decisions in handling market volatility to get results in customer satisfaction

Begin growth

- If you have to understand Customer correctly and Customer has to communicate clearly then increase interaction based improvement in different business strategies from the beginning itself as preparation for fulfillment of smart Innovative competition, to be part of learning and business changes.

V factor

- Volunteer networks could look at business changes with Innovation of the kind
- Value of the community in preserving services
- Volatility of competition for your Innovation
- View of Customer in different processes
- Volume change is more important than output in tourism industry.

Deciphering the user

- Market research and development ventures around growth of social networks could teach employees to understand Customer better because anyway they are in constant results evaluation race on avoiding interference of technology at mastering the hierarchy.

Burning issues

- More details about Customer transition of experience, need and culture can grow better solutions for the continued cooperation of different business resources to right knowledge of its critical issues like technology resistance, research management, employee Innovation and challenges in market.

Extended questions

- Do your own options account for the given need and continued value of Customer in tourism industry?

- Can we get to know about Business offerings better and beforehand to avoiding information to customers after they are ready?

Best efficiency mode

- Technology is no easy way of making efficiency without the help of Customer as visitors to use that tool against combating some or all of the challenges arising in meeting the demand or need.

Minimum bid

- Is no money limits of business investment in customer information or initiatives that become part of global solutions for success of exciting economic prosperity avenues but minimum bid is a good product start for renovation of tourism industry that is too much of services for tourists.

What rules

- In tourism industry emotional value of business services to visitors can get more important than product or Technology to be taken as inherent needs of your business credibility in providing the best experience and value to global network of users of transportation, accommodation etc.

Tie up tourist

- To connect in the process of establishing a good attempt or experience to yield right inputs for the next project tying various cultures of Customer who is no stranger but foreign tourists.

Hi-tech àgility or capability

- Use technology that is formless in gelling of Customer intuitive habit with easy workflow and action in new offerings better to be replaced by inherent capability of Customer in making the tourist life easy.

Running growth

- Growth of tourism industry could be learnt on web and research results but managing fast arrival or change of growth to maturity or decline or saturation can get possible by advanced customisation, inviting Customer interaction, product innovation or decision Verity in encouraging environment of supply chain growth.

Tourism

- In global terms the direct impact is not less than 2.5 trillion dollars, more than tripling for indirect and induced sectors
- The contribution to GDP is not less than 10%
- Is a good contribution to pollution and green house effects.

Sectoral turns

- Utility of tourism development comes from Customer experience in extended future by feeling impact of past visit on occuring behaviour or other without direct correlation but at unexpected change within the industry.

Tourist evaluates

- The changes in culture
- The different countries
- The level of Innovation
- The market improvement
- Customer vs technology involvement

Difference

- Other sectors work with defined boundaries for new demand made by user
- Tourist never puts the demands on different countries but could approve or reject certain obstacles or facilities as faced across visits.

By success

- Buy business success by Customer commitment, not Technology investment for gains counted on sales that boomerang with bye for lack of trust and loyalty of both sides of business and Customer because tourism industry is no dependent on need but could continue with opportunity created by self fulfilling tourists.

Tourist factors

- Treatment from start in online information to in-person interaction to reaching back home for reasons of sharing memory or stories or other unfavourable experience and general perceptions are in tying up with each hidden factor for tourism industry growth.

5Ts in tourism

- Technology perfection
- Teaching visitor psyche
- Timed Innovation
- Temporary adaptation
- Team networks

User in tourism

- Tourist evaluates business with reference to external environment before making decisions in internal environment of fulfillment by associating needs in former impacting market and competitors though users have different wants in their environment.

Corner

- Tourist industry grows big for corners connecting changes, Customers and economy depending upon localisation and customisation of conditions where experience value should be free without asking by the visitors.

Green bay

- Tourism is blue ocean with green bay of plenty of Customer inclinations to cultural offering instead of environmentally deteriorating Business offerings where company can avoid artificial ingredients.

Mindful Strategy

- The market seeks services in mindful and kindful Strategy of optimisation of Customer interaction with most cases for foreign Customers who want to stay in tourism experience of positive terms.

Visitor worth

- The worth of global tourist is immense, in fact that hassle of human interest in other countries is not less when they could create more important quality time with their family at home but they have accepted trouble to visit a nation.

Tourist gives

- Goodwill to your national service
- Preferences for your national prosperity
- Directions to future hospitality
- Motivation to get new ideas for natural resource replenishment.

Tax

- Don't make it taxing for visitors to be vexed in their entertainment pursuits
- Don't tax visitors financially and design business solutions wisely or Innovatively
- Visitors can get hassle free treatment in honour of their cultural opportunity.

- In their country visitors can grow better solution for all problems by home but not as foreigners in another's so the goal of tourism development should be convenient experience for all whether you're foreign or local visitors.

Package

- Hygiene, social, luxury, basic, lifestyle, cultural, daily and ad-hoc needs
- Emphasis on visitor demands or special wishes with safety and entertainment in the two extremes of your business deliverables for your tourism Innovation.

Interrelated

- Tourism should draw lines and expectations for supporting industry in accepting the solution on satisfaction of Customer in different goals from safety to entertainment, visitors should not be shown that dependency but essentially some seamless chain of value across the experience.

Cash on hospitality

- No returns could give good reason for profit as favor from Customer in different places for looking forward to your service or similar for your skill of promoting delight in every business transaction, experience and service.

Capture social media

- Collective interaction with different customers as implementation of goals and solutions for visitors from different nations can grow social media leadership with àgility driven relevance to further pragmatism for visitor motivation.

Nice niche

- Tourist expects freedom of information, communication and entertainment in a way of making comfort on the one visit as it feels so it is more niche and real-time than other sectors, preparation may be more of visitor psyche than business changes.

Revenue

- Tourist spends without much knowledge of the best value, based on first offer, partial bargain, budget restrictions or currency conversion comparison with local or international industry promoting business revenue of multiple possibilities.

Accumulation

- Tourist accumulates treasure of culture tied to new opportunities from world and industry accountability is not unwanted in advance acceptance of positive signal times with future age growth environment.

Ad revenue

- Ad is best for direct visitor experience in tourism because they deserve to add to natural basket of heritage, relics, resources, benefits or other forms of tourist Offering more of which can never be discovered or labelled in ads though packages earn another customer and their investment.

www.ingramcontent.com/pod-product-compliance
Lightning Source LLC
Chambersburg PA
CBHW020555220526
45463CB00006B/2315